How to Read
A Spiritual Book

Kathryn Cousins
Ewert Cousins
Richard J. Payne

PAULIST PRESS
New York/Ramsey

Cover Photo: Morris Berman

Copyright © 1981 by the Missionary Society of St. Paul the Apostle in the State of New York

All rights reserved. No part of this book may be reproduced or transmitted in any form or by any means, electronic or mechanical, including photocopying, recording or by any information retrieval system without permission in writing from the publisher.

ISBN: 0-8091-2415-7

Published by Paulist Press
545 Island Road, Ramsey, N.J. 07446

Printed and bound in the
United States of America

CONTENTS

HOW TO READ A SPIRITUAL BOOK 5
   Meditation 7
   Contemplation 8
   Reading the Bible 12
   Symbolic Interpretation 13
   The Philosophy and Theology
     of Spiritual Reading 17

THE GREAT SPIRITUAL BOOKS PROGRAM 21
   The Classics of Western Spirituality 21
   Study Guides and Discussion Groups 23
   The Spiritual Journey 24
   Classics from Other Traditions 26

Authors of This Volume

KATHRYN and EWERT COUSINS both have doctoral degrees from Fordham University, she in English literature and he in philosophy. She is the indexer of the Classics of Western Spirituality and a developer of the Great Spiritual Books Program. Professor of theology at Fordham University, he is the chief editorial consultant for the Classics. They reside with their three children in Bethlehem, Connecticut.

RICHARD J. PAYNE is the editor-in-chief of the Classics of Western Spirituality. He was born in Ottawa, Canada where he studied science, philosophy and theology at the University of Ottawa. After completing studies in education at the University of Loyola in Chicago, he worked as a supervisor in the Ottawa school system. His career in publishing began in 1967 with Paulist Press. In the fall of 1980 he became Associate Publisher of the Crossroad Publishing Company in New York. He resides with his wife Patricia and their four children in Warwick, New York.

HOW TO READ A SPIRITUAL BOOK

How many hours a week do we spend reading? We read newspapers and magazines for information and relaxation. During our business day we read data sheets, reports, or instructions for operating machines. In the evening we may read a novel or a murder mystery for entertainment. How impoverished our lives would be without reading! It refreshes, relaxes and entertains; it increases our awareness so that we can live life more fully; it provides wisdom for the present and guidance for the future.

We read to be informed, educated, enriched, entertained. But do we ever think about reading to nourish our spiritual life? Our inner life, a priceless possession, needs nourishment from many sources—prayer, worship *and* spiritual reading. Through the centuries countless persons have enriched their spiritual lives by reading great spiritual classics. If we spend time reading for a variety of other purposes, certainly we should read to enhance our spiritual life.

We read a spiritual book differently from other books. In the case of a spiritual book, we read not primarily for information or relaxation, but to open ourselves to a deeper level of reality: to become aware of the sacred, of God's presence and his working in our lives. That means that we must read a spiritual book prayerfully, at a slow pace and with a meditative cast of mind. We should not rush through the text to gather facts, as we would in a newspaper, but move prayerfully through the text into God's presence and the vital flow of our spiritual lives. So much of our reading is geared to gathering facts that we may have to retrain ourselves to read a spiritual book properly.

HOW TO READ A SPIRITUAL BOOK

We begin by realizing that a spiritual book is not a storehouse of information, but a doorway into another realm. The key that opens that door is a prayerful attitude. With that key we can unlock the text and pass into vital contact with its meaning, which is the reality of God and our journey into him.

Spiritual reading has its historical roots in *lectio divina*, a method of prayerful reading that has been practiced in the monastic tradition for centuries. *Lectio divina*, which in Latin means divine reading, has always been part of the daily schedule of the monastery. Each day the monks spend an hour or two or more privately reading Scripture or some spiritual book in a prayerful manner. The key to the method is its slow pace. The monks read very slowly, sometimes aloud, sometimes in silence or forming the words silently with their lips. Their goal is not to finish a passage, but to enter prayerfully into its depths by dwelling on a sentence, a phrase or even a word: mulling over it, ruminating on it, allowing it to sink into their being and resonate on many levels of meaning. The monks are instructed that if something strikes them, they are to pursue it, moving from the text into meditation, affective prayer, and contemplation—in the Latin terms: *meditatio, oratio, contemplatio*.

As this method has been practiced since the early centuries, it has not been directed to one prayerful attitude alone, for example, meditation. Rather it has provided a gateway into many such attitudes evoked spontaneously in the course of the reading. For example, the reader might move from the text to meditate on a specific point, which would lead to spontaneous affective prayer of praise, gratitude, or petition. This in turn might lead to a contemplative attitude: a wondrous gaze, a loving response, or a silent dwelling in the divine presence. After this, the reader might return to the text, letting a word or a phrase draw him directly into the silent presence.

Although many centuries have elapsed since *lectio divina* was developed, it can still provide the basic method for reading spiritual books today. In view of this, it would be wise to explore some of the prayerful attitudes evoked by *lectio divina* as these have been defined in the course of history. It would be helpful also to cite examples of spiritual books that are oriented to specifically different prayerful attitudes: for example, meditation or contemplation.

A distinction is made between meditation and contemplation in *The Mystical Ark* of Richard of St. Victor. One of the most highly esteemed psychologists of the spiritual life, Richard claims that meditation examines an object and contemplation marvels at it. He defines the terms as follows: "Contemplation is a penetrating and free gaze of a soul extended everywhere in perceiving things; but meditation is a zealous attention of the mind, earnestly pursuing an investigation concerning something. Or thus: Meditation is the careful gaze of the soul employed ardently in a search for truth" (p. 157).* Meditation is goal-oriented and proceeds with energy and focus toward what it seeks. As Richard says, "Meditation presses forward with great activity of soul, often through arduous and rough places, to the end of the way it is going. Contemplation, in free flight, circles around with marvelous quickness wherever impulse moves it" (p. 155).

Meditation

Through the centuries meditation was developed as a distinct form of prayer with considerable precision of method. In the Franciscan milieu of the thirteenth century, devotion to the humanity of Christ flourished. This produced a desire to meditate on the concrete historical details of the life of Christ in order to draw out a moral lesson. A classic example of this type of meditation is found in *The Tree of Life* of Bonaventure, the thirteenth century theologian and spiritual writer. With a symbol drawn from Scripture, Bonaventure presents the life of Christ as the Tree of Life, on whose branches blossom twelve fruits, which include such virtues as humility, piety, patience, and constancy presented to us for imitation.

In his meditation on the birth of Christ, Bonaventure summarizes the Gospel accounts of the nativity, choosing details that draw into focus the virtues of poverty and humility: "Although he was great and rich, he became small and poor for us. He chose to be born away from a home in a stable, to be wrapped in swaddling clothes, to be nourished by virginal milk and to lie in a manger between an ox and an ass" (p. 128). Through vivid details, Bonaventure paints a graphic scene and even draws us as participants into the drama of the event. In the following passage, notice how he evokes a response of love for the infant, then elicits contemplative

---

*All references are to Paulist Press' Classics of Western Spirituality editions.

admiration at the host of angels and calls forth a prayer of praise: *Glory to God in the highest* (Lk. 2:14). Thus he passes over from meditation to prayer—blending in the classic method of *lectio divina* the three prayerful attitudes summed up in the Latin terms *meditatio, contemplatio, oratio:*

> Now, then, my soul,
> embrace that divine manger;
> press your lips upon and kiss the boy's feet.
> Then in your mind
> keep the shepherds' watch,
> marvel at the assembling host of angels,
> join in the heavenly melody,
> singing with your voice and heart:
> *Glory to God in the highest
> and on earth peace
> to men of good will.*

This method was given another expression in the *Meditations on the Life of Christ*, which grew out of the early Franciscan tradition and which was erroneously attributed to Bonaventure. These meditations were incorporated into the work of Ludolf of Saxony, which was read by Ignatius of Loyola, who built this form of meditation into his *Spiritual Exercises*. In the hands of Ignatius meditation was worked into a formal method. In the tradition of Richard's goal-oriented definition of meditation, Ignatius elaborated a method of applying the three faculties of memory, understanding, and will, especially to scenes from the life of Christ, from which moral lessons would be derived. As in the case of Bonaventure, this method led also to contemplative wonder and to spontaneous affective prayer. In fact, Ignatius used the term "contemplation" for his meditations on the life of Christ which were less sharply focused on a specific goal.

Contemplation

Examples of contemplation can be found in *The Mystical Ark* of Richard of St. Victor. Through the symbol of the building of the Ark of the Covenant, he leads the reader through six stages of contemplation: from the material world to the soul and to God.

HOW TO READ A SPIRITUAL BOOK

He contemplates each of these three realms from two points of view, thus totaling six stages. On the level of matter, for example, he stands in wonder at "the working of nature, as in grasses, in trees and in animals: in grasses, how they grow and mature; similarly in trees, how they leaf out, blossom and bear fruit; in animals, how they conceive and give birth, how some grow and others die" (p. 180).

Astute psychologist that he is, Richard is especially struck with wonder as he contemplates the human soul: "Come to know your worth, O man, I beseech you; think about the excellent nature of your soul, how God made her according to His image and similitude, how He elevated her above every corporeal creature" (p. 240). He turns the soul around like a multi-faceted diamond, contemplating its varied activities: "Who is not terrified," he asks, "in the wonder of his consideration if he pays careful attention to that fluency of human thinking which is so manifold; the speed of it that is so restless and indefatigable, that runs through so many, such varied and such an infinite number of things; that keeps quiet for neither an hour nor a moment of time, that passes through so great an expanse of space or so great a duration of time in so much haste?" (pp. 250–251). Richard's greatest wonder arises in contemplating God himself. He describes how "the contemplative soul, going beyond not only the corporeal but even the spiritual creation by means of a sublime consideration, is suspended in wonder at the supreme Unity and Trinity" (p. 300).

These same stages of contemplation are found in Bonaventure's *The Soul's Journey into God.* In the spirit of Francis of Assisi's "Canticle of Brother Sun," Bonaventure contemplates the reflection of God in the material world and in our act of sensation. He then moves to contemplate the reflection of God in the soul, in its natural faculties and reformed by grace. He then contemplates God as divine Unity and as the Trinity. Bonaventure adds a seventh stage in which we pass from intellectual contemplation to pure affectivity: from understanding and wonder to love and union. "In this passing over," he says, "if it is to be perfect, all intellectual activities must be left behind and the height of our affection must be totally transferred and transformed into God" (p. 113). This is the contemplation of pure love, in which the soul, without the use of the imagination or the intellect, is united to God by love alone. "But if you wish," Bonaventure says, "to know how these things come about, ask grace

HOW TO READ A SPIRITUAL BOOK

not instruction, desire not understanding, the groaning of prayer not diligent reading, the Spouse not the teacher, God not man, darkness not clarity, not light but the fire that totally inflames and carries us into God by ecstatic unctions and burning affections. This fire is God and *his furnace is in Jerusalem* (Is. 31:9)" (p. 115).

This contemplation of pure affectivity is described in another classic: *The Cloud of Unknowing*. The author of this work takes his method from *The Mystical Theology* of the Pseudo-Dionysius, the method of negating all images and concepts of God. This leads the Pseudo-Dionysius into an emptying of the mind in which God is present in silence and darkness. For the author of *The Cloud*, this emptying leads the soul to a state of union with God in love: "No man can think of God himself. Therefore, it is my wish to leave everything that I can think of and choose for my love the thing that I cannot think." He emphasizes the immediacy of love: "God can be taken and held by love but not by thought." It is good at times to ponder God's kindness and worthiness. "Though this is a light and a part of contemplation, nevertheless, in this exercise, it must be cast down and covered over by a cloud of forgetting." You must step beyond thought and with "love strive to pierce that darkness above you." You are to strike through "that thick cloud of unknowing with a sharp dart of longing love" (Ch. 6).

Some spiritual books are cast largely in the form of prayers addressed directly to God or to Jesus, rather than in the form of meditation or contemplation. These prayers usually evoke strong affectivity, especially love, gratitude and repentance. A classic example of such prayers is found in *The Way of Christ* by Jacob Boehme. Throughout the text there are prayers like the following:

> O highest Love, You have appeared in me. Remain in me. Embrace me in Yourself. Keep me in You so that I cannot bend from You. Fill my hunger with Your love. Feed my soul with heavenly being and give it as drink the blood of my Redeemer Jesus Christ. Let it drink from Your fountain (p. 49).

It would be natural to read such a passage first as a prayer, as it is intended, allowing the words to awaken in you the love and desire for God that they express. In the mood of *lectio divina*,

HOW TO READ A SPIRITUAL BOOK

you might wish to return to the prayer, reading the words slowly, allowing them to draw you into a meditation on the love of God and the meaning of drinking the blood of Jesus in this context. Meditation can lead to contemplation, a wondrous gaze at the mystery of God's love. This can draw you back to the prayer itself, which you can read slowly again and perhaps through it be drawn into the presence of God's love, where you can dwell in silence, without words and without concepts.

Some spiritual books are very practical, providing advice on organizing one's time for prayer and giving direction for the practice of virtue in concrete circumstances. For example, William Law outlines a program of prayer in his work *A Serious Call to a Devout and Holy Life*. Answering an objection that busy working people do not have time to pray throughout the day, he says: "Merchants and tradesmen, for instance, are generally ten times further engaged in business than they need, which is so far from being a reasonable excuse for their want of time for devotion that it is their crime and must be censured as a blamable instance of covetousness and ambition" (p. 281). The problem of setting aside time for prayer still exists—perhaps even more so today than in Law's eighteenth century England. In the face of concrete advice, the reader can consider such suggestions prayerfully, discerning their wisdom and appropriateness for his own style of life.

In reading spiritual books, then, you can begin with the method of *lectio divina*. From the slow reading of the text you can move spontaneously to meditation, affective prayer, or the various forms of contemplation. There is no need to remain in any one of these prayerful attitudes, but you might move from one to the other as the matter suggests or your response leads you. Remember, too, that certain works evoke one attitude more centrally than the others. For example, Bonaventure's *The Tree of Life* begins with the meditative attitude focused on the virtues of Christ's life, but it also moves to prayer and contemplation. Richard of St. Victor's *The Mystical Ark* and Bonaventure's *The Soul's Journey into God* are manuals of contemplation, although they evoke meditation and prayer. As Richard of St. Victor says, the same object can be approached from the standpoint of meditation and the standpoint of contemplation. *The Cloud of Unknowing* presents us with a method of contemplation whereby we can move by negation from meditiation and intellectual contemplation to the contemplation of pure love.

HOW TO READ A SPIRITUAL BOOK

A similar method is presented by the Psuedo-Dionysius in *The Mystical Theology*, with more emphasis on the contemplation of darkness and silence than explicitly on that of love. These latter two works are treatises on the method of contemplation. We can read them to gain instruction in the art of contemplation, it is true; but we can also read them as *lectio divina*, in which we allow ourselves to follow the method, exercising the prayerful attitude of the contemplation of love, silence and darkness.

Reading the Bible

The primary source of spitirual reading has always been Scripture. In the monastic tradition, *lectio divina* was directed chiefly to reading passages from Scripture, although works of the Fathers and other texts were also used. The series The Classics of Western Spirituality does not include an edition of the Bible since this is so widely available. However, reading of Scripture should be the basis of one's own plan for Spiritual reading. This can be realized in several ways: First, you can spend time regularly in the prayerful reading of passages from Scripture. Second, you can weave Scripture reading into your reading of classics from the spirituality tradition. For example, at the beginning and end of your selection for the day, you might read a short passage from Scripture. Third, you can encounter Scripture in the texts of the classics themselves, since they are grounded in Scripture and quote Scripture throughout. Many of them are actually systematic interpretations or meditations on Scripture, such as *The Life of Moses* by Gregory of Nyssa, *The Sermons on the Song of Songs* by Bernard of Clairvaux, and *The Tree of Life* by Bonaventure.

The classics of spirituality can instruct us on how to read Scripture. For example, if we wish to read passages from the Gospels, Bonaventure's *The Tree of Life* can instruct us on how to read the life of Christ meditatively, drawing from it moral lessons for our own life. At the same time it can lead us into contemplation and spontaneous affective prayer. Or we might read the Gospel accounts of Christ's passion in the light of Julian of Norwich's reflections on her vision of the dying Christ as presented in her work entitled *The Showings*. There she describes in vivid detail the vision granted to her of Christ dying on the cross: "I saw the red blood running down from under the crown, hot and flowing freely and copiously, a living stream, just as it was at the time when the crown of thorns was pressed on his blessed head." In this vivid scene, Julian saw the connection with the mystery of the Trinity: "For the Trinity is God, God is the Trinity. The Trinity is our maker, the Trinity is our protector, the Trinity is our everlasting lover, the Trinity is our endless joy and our bliss, by our Lord Jesus Christ and in our Lord Jesus Christ. And this was revealed in the first vision and in them all, for where Jesus appears the blessed Trinity is understood" (p. 181).

Symbolic Interpretation

How is Scripture used in the classics of spirituality? Certainly in many ways. But most consistently Scripture is interpreted symbolically. It may come as a surprise—even a shock—to see how spiritual writers turn to the symbolic interpretation of Scripture to discover its meaning for the spiritual life. In the light of the classics, we can say that symbolic interpretation is the royal road into the spiritual meaning of Scripture. This may present an obstacle to the contemporary reader, for in the twentieth century we have become very literal-minded. We have been conditioned by science, technology, and the importance of facts for history, sociology, and politics. Even in our study of Scripture in the twentieth century, we look for a literal meaning: not so much in terms of the text itself, but in terms of what the text meant in its historical and cultural setting to both the writer and the community out of which it emerged and for which it was intended. Even though Scripture often interprets itself symbolically, this fact does not lead us, as it did the classic spiritual writers, to interpret Scripture symbolically in relation to the spiritual life.

The spiritual writers did not look upon a symbolic interpretation of Scripture as a flight of fancy, a second-best, weak and superficial interpretation as compared with the literal meaning. Quite the contrary; although they rooted themselves in the literal meaning, they thought that this was only the first step, that the more significant meaning of Scripture could be explored only through a symbolic interpretation. This high esteem for symbols is not lacking even in our literal-minded twentieth century, for it is shared by artists, poets and many psychologists, especially of the psychoanalytic schools. In approaching, then, the symbolic interpretation of Scrip-

HOW TO READ A SPIRITUAL BOOK

ture in the spiritual classics, it is important to realize that we may have to begin by overcoming a prejudice.

The spiritual writers not only esteemed and employed the symbolic interpretation of Scripture, they also developed a theory and method for such interpretation. By the High Middle Ages, this was known as the fourfold interpretation of Scripture: (1) the literal, (2) the allegorical, (3) the moral, and (4) the anagogic. The literal meaning is what the text intends to say directly; the allegorical meaning refers to how an event or person in the Old Testament foreshadows Christ; the moral meaning relates to the life of virtue and perfection; the anagogic meaning refers to fulfillment in heaven. Writing in the fourteenth century, after these categories had been clearly worked out by theologians, Dante gave an example of the fourfold interpretation of Scripture in order to illustrate how he intended that his own great work *The Divine Comedy* should be interpreted symbolically. He chose a text from the Psalms which refers to the exodus of the chosen people from Egypt, their passage over the Red Sea, and their taking possession of the promised land. On the literal level he claimed that the text referred to the historical event of the exodus. On the allegorical level, it symbolized the passage of Christ from death to resurrection in his act of redeeming the human race. On the moral level it symbolized the passage of the soul from sin to grace, and, on the anagogic level, the passage of the soul from this life to heaven.

Such an interpretation is by no means arbitrary. The exodus from Egypt to the promised land was a great transformation for the Jewish people. It brought them from slavery to freedom, from repression to fulfillment. Each year they recalled that event in their Passover ritual. It is not surprising, then, that it became the symbol for all transformations in subsequent Jewish and Christian history. In the Christian vision, for example, on the cosmic level the great transformation occurs in the restoration from sin brought about by Christ's redeeming death and resurrection. On the level of the human person, the chief transformation in this life is from sin to grace, and, in the next, the passage from this world to heaven. The spiritual writers were especially perceptive of these transformations and of the objects, events and persons in Scripture that could express them symbolically. They often took a symbolic meaning already expressed in Scripture and developed it more fully.

HOW TO READ A SPIRITUAL BOOK

In this way, through symbols they brought into the spiritual life the rich resources contained in Scripture.

An example of the interpretation of the exodus on the moral level can be found in *The Life of Moses* of Gregory of Nyssa. Referring to the crossing of the Red Sea, he says: "For who does not know that the Egyptian army—those horses, chariots and their drivers, archers, slingers, heavily armed soldiers, and the rest of the crowd in the enemies' line of battle—are the various passions of the soul by which man is enslaved?" He goes on to specify his symbolic meaning: "For the undisciplined intellectual drives and the sensual impulses to pleasure, sorrow, and covetousness are indistinguishable from the aforementioned army. Reviling is a stone straight from the sling and the spirited impulse is the quivering spear point. The passion for pleasures is to be seen in the horses who themselves with irresistible drive pull the chariot" (p. 83).

Gregory's entire treatise is a symbolic interpretation of Scripture. He first summarizes the life of Moses as recorded in Scripture, then he seeks out "the spiritual understanding which corresponds to the history in order to obtain suggestions of virtue" (p. 33). He presents Moses as an example for us, drawing rich symbolic meaning about the life of virtue, such as we saw above. Although his symbolic interpretation is chiefly on the moral level, he deals as well with the other two levels: the allegorical and the anagogic.

Echoing Gregory's treatment of Moses, Richard of St. Victor in his treatise *The Twelve Patriarchs* gives a moral interpretation of the account of the sons of Jacob. For example, he treats Joseph as a symbol of discretion and Benjamin as a symbol of contemplation. In his companion treatise entitled *The Mystical Ark*, he continues the moral interpretation through the symbol of the ark of the covenant. At the outset, he indicates that he is following the moral, not the allegorical interpretation: "The mystical meaning of the ark in the allegorical sense, that is, as it represents Christ, has been articulated by learned persons and investigated by more penetrating minds before. Despite this, we do not presume to be guilty of carelessness by now saying something about it in the moral sense" (p. 151). By "moral" here he intends not the virtues which he examined in *The Twelve Patriarchs*, but the stages of contemplation, which he sees symbolized in the building of the ark.

One of the most cultivated examples of the symbolic approach

HOW TO READ A SPIRITUAL BOOK

is found in the interpretation of the Song of Songs. In the third century Origen laid the foundation for this tradition in his *Commentary on the Song of Songs*, in which he interpreted the bridegroom symbolically as Christ, the Word. He interpreted the bride in two ways: as symbolizing the individual soul and as symbolizing the Church. In the prologue he states: "This book seems to me an epithalamium, that is, a wedding song, written by Solomon in the form of a play, which he recited in the character of a bride who was being married and burned with a heavenly love for her bridegroom, who is the Word of God." He then indicates the two symbolic meanings of the bride. "For whether she is the soul made after his image or the Church, she has fallen deeply in love with him" (p. 217).

Through the centuries many spiritual writers followed Origen's symbolic interpretation in their own commentaries on the Song of Songs. In the twelfth century, Bernard made this the theme of his *Sermons on the Song of Songs*, which is considered one of the masterpieces of the genre. In the hands of a great spiritual master like Bernard, the symbolic interpretation becomes a framework for an exploration of the entire spiritual life. He traces the movement of the soul through the phases of growth to the final stage of union with Christ, which he designates as the "kiss of the mouth."

This symbolism is found richly developed in John of the Cross and Teresa of Avila. In *The Interior Castle*, the latter blends the scriptural symbolism with her own. She bids us to "consider our soul to be like a castle made entirely out of a diamond or of very clear crystal, in which there are many rooms, just as in heaven there are many dwelling places" (p. 35). She then leads us through the castle of the soul until we come to the seventh area which is the dwelling place of Christ, the spouse of the soul. It is here that the mystical marriage is consummated. "When our Lord is pleased," she says, "to have pity on this soul that he has already taken spiritually as his spouse because of what it suffers and has suffered through its desires, he brings it, before the spiritual marriage is consummated, into his dwelling place, which is this seventh" (p. 173).

As we read the classics, we will be guided by the spiritual writers in the symbolic interpretation of Scripture. From them we can learn the method and cultivate its practice. If we can open our souls to the symbolic meaning of Scripture, we will enormously enrich our spiritual life, especially our prayer life. Alerted and trained by the spiritual classics, we can open our *lectio divina* to the symbolic meaning of Scripture. For example, we can read a verse of Scripture like the verse of the Psalm about the exodus, cited by Dante. In the slow, contemplative mood of *lectio divina*, we can let the verse resonate on all four levels of meaning. Allow your own symbolic faculty to awaken and respond to the text. Remember that this symbolic faculty is shaped and trained by the spiritual classics. With their guidance, we can explore the length and breadth, the height and the depth of the mysteries contained in Scripture.

The Philosophy and Theology of Spiritual Reading

The philosophy and theology of reading spiritual books is taken from the symbol of the book. A spiritual book is a mirror of the soul because it reflects the itinerary of the spiritual journey imprinted in the soul. From this point of view, we can look at the soul itself as a book and speak of reading the book of the soul. Spiritual writers have read the book of the soul directly and expressed what they have seen there in their own spiritual books. This notion of "reading the book of the soul" suggests a comprehensive world view based on the symbol of the book, of which reading a spiritual book is only a part. This world view was explicitly developed by Christian spiritual writers in the Middle Ages, for example, Hugh of St. Victor and Bonaventure.

Not only the soul but the entire universe can be looked upon as a book, for it is an expression of God himself. Drawing from a text of the Apocalypse, the spiritual writers call the universe "the book written without," that is, outside the divinity; the meaning of this book is found in "the book written within," that is, within the life of the Trinity. The Trinity itself is like a book, for it is the mystery of the divine expressiveness. From all eternity the divinity wells up in the person of the Father, expressing himself in his Son, his Image and Word, who is united to the Father in the love of the Holy Spirit. The Son, then, as Image and Word of the Father, is "the book written within." This book is eternal, complete, perfect; it contains the meaning of all other books. The Greek term for the Word is Logos, or meaning. From this point of view, the Logos is the expressed Meaning of the Father and

HOW TO READ A SPIRITUAL BOOK

the Meaning expressed in all other books: the book of nature, the book of the soul, the book of Scripture and spiritual books.

The same divine impulse that produced the book written within overflows in producing the book written without. Although the Word is complete on the level of the divinity, God can express himself further on the level of creation. The book written within, then, has its outer expression in the book written without: namely, in the book of creation. When we read the book of creation in its depth, we touch the Word, which is its ultimate Meaning. The book of creation reflects the Word in a variety of ways according to the variety of creatures. The book of creation can be divided into two volumes: the book of nature and the book of the soul. The book of nature, or the material world, reflects the Trinity as its vestige, for it bears the imprint of the Trinity in its power, wisdom, and goodness, which reflect the Father, Son, and Holy Spirit. In a special way creatures reflect the Word, for the Word contains the divine ideas of all that God can create. Each creature is an expression of a divine idea conceived in the Word from all eternity. Each creature, then, can be viewed as an individual word expressing a divine idea, or facet of the eternal Word. In this way the world is like a medieval manuscript copied from its eternal Exemplar. If we can read this manuscript correctly, we can discern its ultimate Meaning, the Word of the Father.

If we turn now to the book of the soul, we see that it not only contains, imprinted in its depths, the itinerary of the spiritual journey but the image of God himself. Through the centuries, spiritual writers have seen in the depths of the soul the reflection of God, who is the Alpha and Omega of the spiritual journey. More precisely, they see the soul reflecting the Word in the Trinity. If we read the book of the soul, then, we discover that it has the same meaning as the book of nature: the Word of the Father. But this meaning is reflected in the book of the soul more directly and intimately than in the book of nature, since the soul, as a spiritual reality with its own interiority, is closer to the divine interiority of the book written within the Trinity.

It is not easy to read the book of nature and the book of the soul. Many are not even aware that nature and the soul are books in this sense. Others who are aware have difficulty reading them in depth. If God produced creation as a book in which we can read the Word of the Father, why do we not discern its meaning

HOW TO READ A SPIRITUAL BOOK

immediately? The spiritual writers tell us why. We are weighed down by sin. Our eyes are clouded and our wills weakened. Darkened by sin, we have lost the capacity to read these books. The book of creation has become foreign to us, as if we hold in our hand a text written in a foreign language, in a foreign alphabet such as Greek or Hebrew, which we cannot decipher. All we perceive are marks on the page whose meaning we do not grasp. As a result, it was necessary that God give us another book: the book of Scripture, to help us read properly the book of nature and the book of the soul. Scripture reminds us that we are the image of God and that creation reflects its Exemplar. It teaches us the divine language we have forgotten. We should turn to the book of Scripture, then, to discover the meaning of the book of nature and the book of the soul; then we can read these three books in relation to one another.

God did not stop with the book of Scripture. He sent us a further expression of himself in the Incarnate Word. The eternal Word in the Trinity—the book written within—united himself to the book written without by assuming human nature in Jesus of Nazareth. This is the ultimate book, the Book of Life, the fullest expression of the divinity in creation, in which all the other books are recapitulated and transformed. In reading this book, we can grasp the meaning of all the other books with clarity and in depth. For the Christian, then, the Word Incarnate is the definitive book, the very presence in human form of the Word as the Meaning of the Father and as the Meaning of the book of nature, the book of the soul, and the book of Scripture.

This interpretation of the image of the book has been part of the continuous Christian tradition. For example, in the early part of the seventeenth century Johann Arndt used the image to provide the structure for his treatise *True Christianity*. He entitled the first part *Liber Scripturae* (the book of Scripture), the second part *Liber Vitae Christus* (the Book of Life, Christ), the third part *Liber Conscientiae* (the book of the soul), and the fourth part *Liber Naturae* (the book of nature). In his reading of the book of nature, for example, Arndt examines the six days of creation as described in Genesis and interprets light symbolically: "Light, in particular the sun," he says, "is a symbol of God and of Christ. It symbolizes God's essence, the most beautiful light, God's eternal wisdom a beam of eternal light, the warm love of God, and the internal spiritual light of the soul that is Christ himself" (p. 233). The whole of Arndt's treatise can be seen as an exercise in reading the various books we have identified here.

Within this world view of the many books, we can situate the reading of spiritual books. These books have been written by persons who have penetrated the meaning of the book of nature, the book of the soul, the book of Scripture, and the Book of Life, the Incarnate Word. Drawing from all of these other books, they cast light upon their meaning. Spiritual books have a purpose beyond themselves: they attempt to make us *readers* in the fullest sense of that term. They sensitize us to read the book of our own souls, to read what can be called "the book of life." As we have used this scriptural term above, it designates the Word in the Trinity. But it can also suggest our own experience of life, which ultimately has its meaning in the Word. By reading spiritual books, we can be trained to live life prayerfully, meditatively, contemplatively—to perceive in the depths of our experience the reflection of eternal Meaning. Having read that meaning in the book of our lives, we can open ourselves to it more completely, respond to its call more profoundly and lead others to it more securely. The spiritual book, then, is a microcosm in which we perceive all the other books and in which their meaning is illumined. To read a spiritual book is to enter into the mystery of that larger reality which is the book written within and without.

THE GREAT SPIRITUAL BOOKS PROGRAM

How, then, do we begin? What books do we choose? Where can we find them? Can we find someone to share our experience of these books? To discuss them with us? Perhaps even to meditate and pray with us? To answer these questions, Paulist Press has introduced The Great Spiritual Books Program. This project is designed to put us in touch with the great spiritual books of Western culture, to assist us in reading them privately and to provide the means for forming discussion groups to explore the works with others.

The Great Spiritual Books Program has three dimensions: (1) the selection of books to read, which are found in the series The Classics of Western Spirituality; (2) the Study Guides accompanying each book, available in 1982, which provide guidance to read the book privately and to form discussion-prayer groups; (3) periodic meetings of the discussion-prayer groups to explore a particular volume with the aid of the Study Guide.

The Classics of Western Spirituality

The first phase of the program addresses the question: What books should we read? That question can be answered very practically now, because of the Paulist Press sixty-volume series entitled The Classics of Western Spirituality. Hailed as "the most hopeful sign in American publishing," the series was enthusiastically received. The volumes have been uniformly praised by critics for the richness of their content, the literary quality of the translations and the scholarly excellence of the editing. Already these volumes

THE GREAT SPIRITUAL BOOKS PROGRAM

have enriched the lives of readers throughout the world, for they are meeting a need for spiritual nourishment that people desperately feel. Readers are discovering that the spiritual life is enormously rich, challenging and exciting—that it is for everyone concerned with loving God. They are finding that spirituality is the very lifeblood of religion, that it is not rigid rules or arid prayer regimes, but a vital reality experienced in the totality of their lives.

The works in the series have been chosen by a board of experts to include the greatest spiritual books of the Western world. Before this series was launched, these works were not easily available. In cases where individual works were published, these were not collected in a single series and were hard to find in bookstores. Even if the reader knew what titles to search for, they were often hidden from him by poor and unappealing translations, by no translations at all, by editions now out of print or by a lack of editions in modern times. Happily this is no longer the case, for the reader can now find in this series the entire range of the spiritual journey as it has been chartered by the masters of Western spirituality.

The series does not limit itself to one tradition, but offers the reader the whole of the Western spiritual quest. In the atmosphere of the late twentieth century, there is a growing interest not only in one's own spiritual tradition but in others as well—and in mankind's spiritual quest as a whole. For this reason, the series includes spiritual traditions in the West that have preceded and paralleled the Christian tradition: American Indian, Afro-American, Jewish, and Islamic. Consciously and unconsciously all of these traditions have formed the modern religious climate and are shaping its future. The series, then, provides classics from these traditions in order to enlarge our horizons to enrich our spiritual wisdom and to equip us for the future.

These books in the series are called classics because they have been written by masters of the spiritual life. Imagine having as our spiritual guide Gregory of Nyssa, Bonaventure, or Teresa of Avila! The authors are the giants of their field; they are not superficial popularizers or writers of sentimental devotion. With God's grace they have lived the spiritual life in depth—even heroically; many have been declared saints. They have not only practiced the spiritual life, but have received the gift of wisdom to share their spiritual insights with others. They have written works that have stood the test of centuries, acknowledged by experts and the com-

THE GREAT SPIRITUAL BOOKS PROGRAM

munity at large as the finest of their genre. These books are classic expressions of their traditions and have an intrinsic authority whether they are ancient, medieval, modern, or contemporary.

Some people may be afraid to read a book labelled "classic." They mistakenly believe that such books will be too "profound," too "advanced" for them to understand. On the contrary, these books are classics precisely because they have appealed to a broad readership. They are not highly technical treatises for experts alone, for advanced ascetics or professional theologians; rather, they were written for ordinary people who were concerned with growing in spiritual awareness and love of God. Through the centuries countless numbers have read them with understanding and profit. Before printing they were copied again and again in manuscript form. After the invention of printing, they were published in many editions. The classics are for everyone. One should not hesitate, then, to open them and plunge in. For guidance into the text, each volume in the series has a preface and introduction. To open up the richness of the text even more fully, The Great Spiritual Books Program offers Study Guides and discussion sessions.

Study Guides and Discussion Groups

The second phase of The Great Spiritual Books Program consists of the use of Study Guides. Each volume in The Classics of Western Spirituality will be accompanied by a Study Guide. This will assist the reader in his own private exploration of the volume and provide groups with material for discussion and prayer. The Study Guide will help the individual find his way into the spiritual riches of each volume of the series. It will provide a prayerful context for his own spiritual reading and then lead him into the major themes of the work and raise questions for his consideration.

Although the Study Guides can aid one in private reading, they are especially designed for group meetings. The spiritual journey is not merely personal; it is a journey with others. It is vitally important that we support, guide and nourish each other along the way. To grow in the spiritual life, we must share with others and receive from them. For this reason The Great Spiritual Books Program culminates in the third phase, which is the group meeting for discussion and prayer based on a specific volume. Each member of the group will bring to the meeting the fruits of his private reading—along with questions, doubts, concerns. The sharing of these will benefit all, providing each with companions and guidance in the spiritual journey.

The groups will meet once a week or every two weeks. They will devote four or six meetings to a specific volume, dividing the material according to the plan outlined in the Study Guide. Each time the group will discuss a different theme, which is developed in an essay in the Study Guide for that meeting.

As presented in the Study Guides, the format of the meeting combines prayer and discussion. The meeting begins with an opening prayer taken from Scripture or some other source. This is followed by spontaneous vocal prayer. The group discusses the theme treated in the essay for that meeting. Questions on the theme are provided in the Study Guide, but it is strongly recommended that members raise their own questions. The meeting closes in a prayerful mood. First, a meditational reading aloud by one of the group, followed by spontaneous vocal prayer and a formal prayer read aloud.

The Spiritual Journey

In its three phases, The Great Spiritual Books Program is designed to awaken us to the spiritual journey and to guide us along the way. Spiritual books deal largely with the spiritual journey. In a number of cases they record a personal journey in the form of an autobiography: for example, *The Confessions* of St. Augustine, or *The Book of Her Life* of Teresa of Avila. Although personal journals and autobiography form a significant genre of spiritual writings, a larger group deals with the spiritual journey in a more general sense. Instead of recording a personal journey, they provide a map of the journey for many to follow. For example, Bonaventure wrote a work entitled *The Soul's Journey into God.* The key Latin word in the title is *itinerarium*, which can be translated "journey," but more precisely "itinerary," or plan of a journey, or map of a journey. The work charts seven stages of contemplation by which the soul proceeds toward union with God. In the same genre, Bonaventure wrote another work entitled *The Triple Way.* The key term in the Latin title is *via*, meaning "way" in the sense of path or road. The path is triple because it leads us in a threefold process of purgation, illumination, and perfection. In the first we are purged of faults, in the second we are illumined by God's grace, and in the third we are united to God. Sometimes a work combines the personal journey with the map of the journey. For example, when Bonaventure wrote his biography of Francis of Assisi, he organized the material of the saint's personal journey according to the map of the universal journey which he had charted in *The Triple Way*.

The journey can be looked upon from many points of view. In addition to the triple way, many writers chart a path through virtues and through stages of contemplation. Progress in the spiritual life involves growth in virtue and growth in prayer, especially contemplative prayer. It is not surprising, then, that authors chart a path through those virtues that lead to contemplative prayer. For example, in *The Twelve Patriarchs* Richard of St. Victor develops with great psychological acumen the interior virtues that bring the soul to the threshold of contemplation: beginning with fear of God, grief, hope of forgiveness, and love of God, proceeding through the internal discipline of our imagination, and moving to discretion and full self-knowledge into contemplation. In a second work, *The Mystical Ark*, Richard continues the spiritual journey, this time through six stages of contemplation that lead to direct, even ecstatic contemplation of God. A similar path is charted by Gregory of Nyssa in *The Life of Moses*, where his symbolic interpretation of events in Moses' life reveals the virtues that lead to the perfection of the Christian life and the heights of contemplative prayer. Teresa of Avila's *The Interior Castle* guides the reader from the outside to the inside of the castle of the soul, charting both virtues and stages of contemplation.

The image of the journey permeates The Classics of Western Spirituality. How should we read such books? Through The Great Spiritual Books Program, we can acquire knowledge of our own spiritual journey. We can learn its direction, its dynamics, its obstacles, its goal. The spiritual classics provide us with a map of the spiritual journey; they sketch our own itinerary. In so doing, they present us with a mirror of our own souls, for they reflect the map of the journey imprinted on each soul. By gazing into this mirror, we become conscious of the fact that our lives at their deepest level contain a spiritual itinerary, according to which God is guiding us toward union with him. We must be awakened to this fact, for the surface events of our lives often cloud our eyes, preventing us from discerning the direction in which God is leading us. We become caught in the daily routine, entrapped by cares, buffeted by our desires and frustrations. We often fluctuate between boredom and anxiety. When joy comes our way, it may not flow from the depths of our being but from some outer event that touches merely the surface of our lives.

Reading spiritual books can awaken us to a whole new dimension of life, for they deal not with the surface, but with the depths. They can awaken us to our own spiritual journey and reveal our own itinerary. They help us to perceive the working of God's grace in our lives so that we will respond to that grace, not turning away from the path God is pointing out, not becoming faint or falling behind. These books open the path for us and guide us along the way. The autobiographies give us concrete examples of how saints proceeded on their own personal journeys. Of course, these saints were given extraordinary gifts of grace and they responded heroically. But in their lofty journey to the heights, we can see reflected the lower path that God has given to us. And in the universal maps which the spiritual writers provide, we can see the outlines of our own itinerary.

Classics from Other Traditions

The Classics of Western Spirituality contains classics from a number of traditions. Within Christianity the major currents are represented: Orthodox, Catholic, Protestant. The series also includes classics from other traditions: Jewish, Islamic, and Native American. This raises questions: Why are these diverse traditions contained in one program? And how can we read a spiritual book from a tradition other than our own? The first question can be answered by pointing to the major historical-cultural development of the late twentieth century. We are in the midst of one of the greatest transformations in history, which is leading us into global consciousness. Over the last several centuries, there has been a constant build-up of population, transportation and communications to the point now that we are developing a planetary civilization with a single global consciousness. At the same time there have emerged the ecumenical movement and the dialogue of world religions, in which the great traditions of spirituality are meeting each other in a mood of openness, respect, and mutual enrichment. All of this is supported by the enormous research into the history of mankind's spiritual quest. At such a moment in history and in such a context, it would

THE GREAT SPIRITUAL BOOKS PROGRAM

be unwise to launch a series that did not reflect this development and that did not prepare its participants for the new global environment of spirituality.

The emergence of global consciousness does not mean that all diversity will be lost in the ocean of the whole. Quite the contrary. Global consciousness means precisely consciousness of diversity. We can no longer move into the future, aware of our own tradition alone. We must see our spiritual quest in relation to the spiritual quest of other traditions and of mankind as a whole. The Classics of Western Spirituality is a step in this direction. The term "Western" is taken both historically and geographically. Historically, it refers to those world religions stemming from Judaism: namely, Christianity and Islam. Although Islam has spread both east and west, its roots lie in the Judaeo-Christian tradition that is the religious basis for Western culture. The choice of American Indian religiosity is geographic, in the sense that its adherents live in North and South America and have interacted with the Judaeo-Christian tradition there.

Against this background, we can address the question: How can we read a spiritual book from a tradition other than our own? First, we should read with an open mind and an open spirit, in the ecumenical mood of the twentieth century. Next, we should listen attentively, allowing the writer to express his spiritual experience on its own terms. We should not read him exclusively from our point of view, filtering everything he says through our own categories. Rather we should attempt to share the point of view of his experience. That means we have to enter into his experience—to empathize with it, to respond to its values, to see the world from his point of view. Only in this way can we be true to his experience and enrich our own experience.

Once we have opened ourselves in this way, as we read prayerfully in the mood of *lectio divina*, we may find ourselves responding to the other tradition from several points of view. We may be struck by what is common to our own tradition, drawing confirmation, support and enrichment from this discovery. We will probably find much in common, for the spiritual journey is strikingly similar even in religions that have marked differences in belief. Because of contrasting emphases, the other tradition may awaken something that has lain hidden in our own tradition. In these cases we will find solidarity with the other tradition, but in other instances we may become aware of differences that separate us—differences that may not be capable of being resolved. These, too, can be enriching, for they highlight what is unique in our own tradition, clarifying the roots of our identity. Having prayerfully encountered the other tradition, we will have a much deeper and more complex relation to its spiritual heritage. Not only will we be enriched spiritually by such an encounter, but we will have grown in that complex, relational consciousness which the future will require of us.

Let us illustrate this encounter from the point of view of a Christian reading books from the Jewish, Islamic, and American Indian spiritual traditions. In works of Jewish spirituality, the Christian will undoubtedly discern the common ground of both traditions in biblical revelation. This will be no new discovery for him, for his own tradition shares the sacred books of Judaism. However, to see this biblical tradition alive in Jewish spirituality may vitalize the Christian's biblical roots. Yet he will probably make a discovery: the Jewish mystical tradition, for this took shape chiefly after the beginning of the Christian era. It is a powerful tradition, one that sees the world flooded with divine light, filled with divine sparks that must be released from entrapment to draw all things into divine unity.

In *Lights of Holiness*, Rabbi Kook observes: "The mystical dimension is the soul of religion, the soul of the Torah. From its substance derives all that is revealed, all that is circumscribed, all that can be conceived by logic, and all that can be carried out in actions" (p. 194). Coming out of a tradition that has often emphasized a flight from the world, the Christian may be pleasantly surprised at the this-wordly emphasis in Jewish mysticism. For example, Rabbi Kook says: "The far-reaching unity of the mystical dimension embraces all creatures, all conditions of thought and feeling, all forms of poetry and exposition, all expressions of life, all aspirations and hopes, all objectives and ideals, from the lowest depths to the highest heights" (p. 195). This-worldly mysticism is cultivated by the Hassidic tradition and stands behind the enigmatic tales of Nahman of Bratslav (p. 33).

For the Chrisitian an Islamic book will probably seem more foreign than a Jewish book. Yet the Christian may find that he is more at home than he anticipated, for when he reads a Sufi work, in the mystical tradition of Islam, he will find the universal aspects of spirituality emphasized more than the specific beliefs of

THE GREAT SPIRITUAL BOOKS PROGRAM

Islam. For example, being liberated from the prison of the false self is a recurrent theme not only in Christian but in world spirituality. In his work entitled *Intimate Conversations*, the Sufi writer Ansari begs: "Give me deliverance from the bonds of my self, O Lord. Give me freedom from my evil self, O Lord" (p. 206).

In Islam the Christian can discover a dimension of his belief in God that is often submerged in his own tradition. Because of the incarnation, the Christian emphasizes the divine immanence rather than transcendence and God's love more than his power. The Muslim, on the other hand, focuses on the overwhelming transcendence and power of Allah. This is at the very heart of his religious experience. While emphasizing the opposite pole, the Christian does not reject God's transcendence and power. Through Islam, then, the Christian can come to a deeper understanding of this side of God and observe how it can vitalize his spiritual life.

As he reads Muslim books, the Christian will be aware of a major difference from Islam. Christ is missing from Islamic spirituality. Although Muslims venerate Christ as a prophet, they completely reject the Christian claim that Christ is the Son of God and Redeemer of the world. To a large measure, Christian spirituality is focused on Christ. Perhaps because of this, Christians have not developed devotion to God as thoroughly as Muslims. For them a central practice is devotion to Allah through his "ninety-nine beautiful names," the attributes assigned to Allah in the Qu'ran such as the designations: merciful, compassionate, just. In *The Book of Wisdom*, Ibn 'Ata' Illah writes of God: "He illumined exterior phenomena with the lights of his created things; and he illumined the innermost hearts with the uncreated lights of his attributes. For that reason, the lights of exterior phenomena set, whereas the lights of hearts—and of the innermost hearts—do not set" (p. 72). By chanting and meditating on these divine attributes, the Muslim awakens the uncreated lights in his innermost heart. Instructed by the Muslim, the Christian can enrich his own spirituality by assimilating the Muslim devotion to the beautiful names of God.

Although the Christian may see the value of reading Jewish and Islamic classics, he may wonder at the wisdom of reading the spirituality of the American Indians. After all, are they not pagan and even primitive—untouched by God's revelation? What value can their spirituality offer? To enter into fruitful dialogue, the Christian will have to change the stereotypes contained in these questions and open himself to the richness of the primitive experience and its religious depth. He will have to realize that in the process of development, the so-called higher civilizations have lost a number of values—and, among these, spiritual values—that have been retained by primitive peoples, such as the American Indians. Moreover, the religions of civilization usually retain a level of symbol and ritual that is more characteristic of the primitive stratum of culture. Often the Christian or Jew will feel alienated from this level of his heritage. By discovering its meaning and value in the American Indians, he can assimilate it in a more organic way into his own tradition.

The American Indians, for example, have a profound sense of the sacrality of nature, of God's presence in the material world, of their own organic unity with the world of animals and plants. Out of this flows a reverence for nature and a pervasive gratitude for all that God has given. In the volume entitled *Native North American Spirituality of the Eastern Woodlands*, a Seneca Thanksgiving Address paints an elaborate picture of the creation of the universe, with plants, animals and humans. It concludes with a powerful statement of gratitude: "And now this is what Our Creator did. He decided 'I myself shall continue to dwell above the sky, and that is where those on the earth will end their thanksgiving. They will simply continue to have gratitude for everything they see that I created on the earth, and for everything they see that is growing.'" The address continues: "'The people moving about on the earth will have love; they will simply be thankful. They will begin on the earth, giving thanks for all they see. They will carry it upward, ending where I dwell'" (p. 67).

It is precisely this sense of gratitude for creation that the technological civilizations have lost. They have exploited the earth and polluted the environment. From the American Indian they can learn that creation is sacred and must be respected as a gift from God. From the Indians also, they can learn the religious significance of symbols drawn from creation and of rituals that celebrate God's gift of nature. In this way, the spirituality of primitive peoples has an abiding place in the emerging planetary culture and must be included along with the great world religions within the emerging global consciousness.

To read classics from other traditions, then, can enrich our spiritual growth. We may not be able to participate fully in these

THE GREAT SPIRITUAL BOOKS PROGRAM

other traditions, but we can share in them at least partially. As we read classics from other traditions, we will come to realize, through a difference in emphasis and perspective, the vastness, the awesomeness of the journey we are on. For we are not on this journey alone, but in the company of all mankind. We will see that this journey has been in progress not only for two or three thousand years, but that it was already undertaken before the dawn of recorded history as the spirituality of primitive cultures attests. As it moves into the future, the new direction of this collective journey is not yet clear. But we can equip ourselves now by not only grounding ourselves in the roots of our own spiritual heritage, but by opening ourselves to the spiritual heritage of mankind as a whole.

For more information on the Paulist Press series
The Classics of Western Spirituality
please write to the Paulist Press, 545 Island Road
Ramsey, N.J. 07446